THE LOS ANGELES 1984 OLYMPIC GAMES

Los Angeles was transformed into the "look" of the 1984 Olympic Games by temporary structures erected to mark the venues and to serve broadcast, lighting, and security functions but mostly to decorate the city for a party. The tallest of all was this 135-foot-high Olympic Tower at the Los Angeles Memorial Coliseum. (Courtesy LA84 Foundation.)

FRONT COVER: Mary Lou Retton became the first female gymnast from outside Eastern Europe to win the Olympic gold medal in the gymnastics individual all-around competition. Called "America's Sweetheart" by the media, her five medals were the most by any athlete at the Games. (Courtesy LA84 Foundation.)

COVER BACKGROUND: Calvin Smith passed the baton to Carl Lewis for the anchor leg of an American world-record performance in the 4x100-meter relay. (Courtesy LA84 Foundation.)

BACK COVER: The Opening Ceremony was set to begin at the Coliseum. (Courtesy LA84 Foundation.)

THE LOS ANGELES 1984 OLYMPIC GAMES

Barry A. Sanders

ARCADIA PUBLISHING

ISBN 978-1-4671-3037-0

Published by Arcadia Publishing
Charleston, South Carolina

Printed in the United States of America

Library of Congress Control Number: 2013932731

For all general information, please contact Arcadia Publishing:
Telephone 843-853-2070
Fax 843-853-0044
E-mail sales@arcadiapublishing.com
For customer service and orders:
Toll-Free 1-888-313-2665

Visit us on the Internet at www.arcadiapublishing.com

This book is dedicated to Marian and Louis Sanders.

CONTENTS

ACKNOWLEDGMENTS

Telling the story of the Los Angeles 1984 Olympic Games 30 years later would not be possible without access to written and photographic records that bring the events back to life with accuracy and immediacy and the help of friends whose memories are sharp and who are generous with their time and patience. I have been most fortunate to have been given access to the exhaustive photographic archives of the LA84 Foundation Sports Library, the official repository of the 1984 Games records, and to the thoughts and memories of those who maintain the records. I thank LA84 Foundation president Anita de Frantz, vice president of communications Wayne Wilson, and manager Shirley Ito for their personal help, advice, and recollections, as well as the images they provided to me.

Richard Perelman, who was editor-in-chief in 1985 of both the *Official Report of Games of the XXIIIrd Olympiad* and *Olympic Retrospective*, was of special help in leading me to good images and in helping assure the accuracy of this account. The publications he edited are the solid base for any discussion of the events of the 1984 Games.

I appreciate the fine work of Jared Nelson, my editor at Arcadia, who suggested I write this book and shepherded it into print.

My wife, Nancy, was my best advisor and enthusiastic partner in this endeavor as in all things that I do.

Most comprehensively I acknowledge and thank the thousands of employees and volunteers of the Los Angeles Olympic Organizing Committee and the thousands of athletes who competed at the Los Angeles 1984 Olympic Games. They created the lasting memories about which we now write and read. I regret that in this concise book it is impossible to identify or depict all of the significant participants, and I apologize to those who are not mentioned by name.

Unless otherwise noted, all images appear courtesy of the LA84 Foundation. Images noted as courtesy of NOPP/*LA Times* are taken from the National Olympic Photo Pool, administered by the *Los Angeles Times*. They all are copyrighted by the *Los Angeles Times*, 1984, and are provided courtesy of the LA84 Foundation pursuant to agreement between them.

INTRODUCTION

The 1984 Games will be remembered by those with clear heads as the 16 days that preserved this rich treasure that brings together more than 200 nations every four years. . . . It saved the Games, gave the USOC a solid financial future, and created a blueprint for the future.

—Michael Moran
US Olympic Committee
Chief Spokesperson and Communications Executive
1979–2003

When the right to host the Games of the XXIIIrd Olympiad, the 1984 Olympic Games, was awarded to Los Angeles in 1978, the Olympic movement was in grave trouble. Montreal had lost over $1 billion in staging the 1976 Games, and the coffers of the International Olympic Committee (IOC) and the US Olympic Committee (USOC) were almost bare. No other city wanted the 1984 Games. Los Angeles recognized that it had the human and physical resources to make the Olympic Games a success where others might fail. It proposed to do the Games differently, with private funding and management and with little new construction. It set out to demonstrate a "Spartan" approach that would shift the spotlight from grandiose arrangements to the athletes and their achievements. The IOC, lacking any alternatives, reluctantly acceded and began a partnership with Los Angeles of increasing cordiality that yielded important athletic and financial success and, more importantly, a new worldwide perception of the Olympic Games as the ultimate validation of a city. The Olympic movement in the United States and globally was put on a new secure budget footing and a new upward trajectory.

For the people of Los Angeles, the Games were a watershed in the image that they and others have had of their unique city. Los Angeles had been the perfect Olympic city for a long time. It hosted the Games of the Xth Olympiad in 1932, which invented the idea of the Olympic Village and had a financial surplus, despite being organized in the Depression. Its year-round temperate climate and geographic variety from the mountains to the sea made it a mecca for athletes and sports activity of all kinds. Consequently, the region has always been home to a greater concentration of Olympians than any other area of the world. Its broad sports enthusiasm meant that Los Angeles already had top-quality facilities for almost the entire range of Olympic events. But the essence of Los Angeles's qualification for the Games was more than its environment and infrastructure: it was the creativity, optimism, and individual initiative that defined the spirit of its millions of people who were and are still its chief assets. They were a mixed population from the far reaches of the world who would respond to the challenge of a great creative project. They built the world's "dream machine" in its entertainment industry and in its aerospace industry. Los Angeles, with its emphasis on individual freedom, imagination, and personal initiative, was and remains the most American of American cities.

The Games almost did not happen. Games promoters in Los Angeles knew that on an operating basis, before accounting for construction costs, prior Olympic Games had been profitable, and they were confident that a combination of increased television revenue and the use of Los Angeles's wealth of existing facilities would avoid the deficits that had plagued earlier Games. But the public was skeptical, worried that it would be asked to pick up the tab. It adopted an initiative called "No Olympic Tax" just as the leaders were engaged in persuading the IOC to award the Games to Los Angeles. Such a measure had caused Denver to lose the 1976 Winter Games after they had been awarded to that city.

The IOC saw the facts in the same way as Los Angeles voters but with contrasting results. The IOC was equally skeptical that there would be no deficit and thus all the more determined to enforce the provisions of its charter requiring the taxpayers to stand behind the Olympic Organizing Committee and pick up the tab. Squaring this circle was the difficult task of the civic leadership of Los Angeles. Through almost a year of negotiation after the Games were provisionally awarded to Los Angeles in May 1978, and in which both sides came very close to canceling the project, a unique arrangement was reached between the IOC and a private Los Angeles nonprofit called the Los Angeles Olympic Organizing Committee (LAOOC), in which the USOC would stand in place of the government as the guarantor of any deficits.

With the suspenseful negotiations over, the LAOOC set to work to stage the Games. First, it hired Peter V. Ueberroth, a man who typified the Los Angeles qualities of private creativity, energy, and success. He assembled a team of mostly young executives from the area who also shared the personality of Los Angeles. They prepared the Games in a way that would be a great celebration while exceeding past revenues and avoiding unnecessary costs. Los Angeles had the expertise to recognize the hidden value in the television rights to the Games. LAOOC auctioned the US rights, awarding them to ABC for $225 million—the largest television rights fee for any show in history and vastly more than the $80 million fee paid for the preceding Games. Of that amount, $33.5 million went to the cash-starved IOC. LAOOC also raised over $125 million from sponsors, suppliers, and licensees to the Games—a more than sixfold increase over the amount raised from similar programs in each of the Montreal 1976 and Moscow 1980 Games. In the end, the Games yielded a surplus of over $232 million that has endowed the USOC and youth sports in Los Angeles in perpetuity.

Some have said that Los Angeles introduced commercialism to the Games. The opposite is true. Both television and sponsorships had been features of the Games for decades. Montreal in 1976 had 166 corporate sponsors and suppliers, and Moscow in 1980 had 225. Los Angeles had only 99 corporate sponsors and suppliers. As to licensees, who paid to use the Games' symbols, Montreal licensed 140 such companies, and Moscow licensed 7,272 such companies, while Los Angeles licensed only 65. LAOOC understood that by granting exclusivity in categories of goods and services to sponsors, suppliers, and licensees, it could gain much higher fees. This reduced commercial clutter while vastly increasing revenue to the Games. Since 1984, the IOC has followed and extended the Los Angeles model and has consistently raised far more revenue than in Los Angeles.

More important than revenue in reaching a financial surplus was LAOOC's lack of construction. Los Angeles was uniquely positioned to do so. It had the venues and housing. It needed to build only three competition sites, a velodrome, a pool, and a shooting range. The presence of such existing facilities was a natural outgrowth of the city's active sports population. Few if any other cities are similarly blessed, so this aspect of the 1984 Games has not yet been replicated.

Still, problems were anticipated. Up until the eve of the Games, the *Los Angeles Times* warned gravely of smog, traffic, and indebtedness. As the Games unfolded, these concerns were proven groundless in an unbroken string of days of clear air and clear freeways and, finally, fiscal success.

On the international scene, problems did arise. The Soviet Union, then the arch-rival of the United States in Olympic competition, was still aggrieved by Pres. Jimmy Carter's boycott of the Moscow 1980 Olympic Games. LAOOC worked hard to avoid a reciprocal boycott. It met frequently with Soviet officials and agreed in 1983 to appoint the USSR's state sporting goods monopoly, Glavsportprom, as the official supplier of the sophisticated electronic equipment needed for the fencing competition. Nevertheless, on May 8, 1984, as the torch relay was beginning in New York City, the Soviet Union announced it would not attend the Games. Then, for two weeks, 14 of its Eastern Bloc allies, one per day, joined the boycott. Strenuous efforts by LAOOC prevented Romania, Yugoslavia, and the People's Republic of China from joining the boycott. When the fencing equipment arrived at the dock, LAOOC sent it back.

Defiantly, LAOOC and all of Los Angeles geared up for a great Olympic Games with or without the boycotters. And great they were. The Opening Ceremony was a television spectacular that became a model for all those that have followed. The 2008 Fou drummers at the Opening Ceremony in Beijing in 2008 had their roots in the 85 pianists playing Gershwin's "Rhapsody in Blue" at the 1984 Games. The ceremonies have grown in ensuing Games, but they have not fundamentally changed from the Los Angeles model.

The athletes, all 7,000 of them, performed in a manner that gave pride to their homelands and inspiration and excitement to the viewers. Sprinter and long jumper Carl Lewis and gymnast Mary Lou Retton were the most recognized of the American team's fleet of gold medalists. Li Ning became a national idol in China for his gymnastics victories. Swimmer Alex Baumann made headlines for Canada. Middle distance runner Sebastian Coe and decathlete Daley Thompson starred for Great Britain. Steffi Graf of Germany and Michael Jordan and Patrick Ewing of the United States excelled in Los Angeles as preludes to renowned professional careers in tennis and basketball, respectively. Moroccan hurdler Nawal el Moutawakel and Portuguese marathoner Carlos Lopes were the first gold medalists in the history of each of their nations. Coe and el Moutawakel later became important leaders in the Olympic movement.

Undeniably, the boycott did dim the quality of competition in some sports, especially weightlifting, where the Eastern Bloc was dominant. As in most Olympic Games, the host nation did better than it would normally do, but American success in winning 174 medals was exaggerated due to the absence of the Soviets and the East Germans. Nevertheless, the majority of sports were highly competitive and exciting and unaffected by the absences. The Games set a new record in team attendance with 140 countries. Some 90 Olympic and 13 world records were set or equaled across many disciplines. The impact of the American medal run was not to lessen the Games but to enhance the growing audience fervor. The home team's success in the competitions added to the sense in Los Angeles that this was the greatest celebration of the era. Those who were there remember the joy. In its afterglow, the exultant USOC took its entire team on a five-city ticker-tape tour ending at the White House.

The global public reaction to the broadcasts from Los Angeles, as well as the financial success, reignited the ambitions of cities everywhere to bid for the Games. The strength of the Olympic movement today is one of the legacies of the 1984 Games. The memories and accomplishments of 1984 and 1932 drive Los Angeles to seek to reproduce the experience once again, in a new way suited for the world and Los Angeles as they have continued to change.

The "Star in Motion" symbol of LAOOC

1

Los Angeles Bids for the Games

Bidding to host the Olympic Games is in Los Angeles's blood. Shortly after the successful Los Angeles 1932 Games, the IOC (through IOC member and American Olympic Association president Avery Brundage) approached the leadership in Los Angeles with the possibility that the 1940 Games, then scheduled for Tokyo, might have to be moved because of the spreading war in Asia. Angelenos responded immediately by offering to stage the Games in Los Angeles and by establishing a new organization, the Southern California Committee for the Olympic Games (the Southern California Committee or SCCOG) to focus their efforts. As the international situation worsened, the 1940 Games were cancelled, but the Southern California Committee became the nation's first and only independent organization devoted to both bidding for the Games and advancing the Olympic movement in general.

Year after year, the Southern California Committee supported the American Olympic team by fundraising and by its annual track-and-field meet. It nurtured relationships with the members of the IOC and began bidding for the Games as soon as the war was over. Mayor after mayor joined with the committee to bid for each quadrennial award. At first, Los Angeles bid directly to the IOC. After the 1956 bids, the rules changed so that the USOC would select one American city to bid each time. For four successive bids, it chose Detroit over Los Angeles as its standard bearer. Detroit was the home of USOC president Doug Roby. For 1976, it finally turned to Los Angeles with a bid that proposed to finance the Games through the sale of television rights. Nevertheless, Montreal was selected by the IOC. Los Angeles tried again for 1980, but Moscow won.

In May 1978, following the financial debacle of the Montreal 1976 Games, Los Angeles was the only bidder for 1984 (after Teheran failed to bid due to its revolution). Los Angeles offered to stage the event under a private organizing committee, financed by privately raised funds, and using the area's wealth of existing facilities—a "Spartan" approach. The IOC reluctantly and conditionally awarded the Games to Los Angeles while insisting on a government guarantee against a deficit. Los Angeles and its population resisted the pressure for taxpayer funding and struggled with the IOC until a guarantee by the USOC sealed the deal in late 1978. The Games would return to Los Angeles.

The inspiration for the 1984 Games arose from the successful Games of the Xth Olympiad, held in Los Angeles in 1932. Those Games invented the Olympic Village. They earned a financial surplus of $1 million in the depths of the Depression, put Los Angeles on the international sports map, and gave birth to the Southern California Committee to support the Olympic movement and to return the Games to Los Angeles.

The Southern California Committee bid at every opportunity. Here is its delegation to the IOC meeting in Stockholm in 1947 in pursuit of the 1952 Games. From left to right are Ralph Chick, John Jewett Garland, William May Garland, Frank Bull, and chairman Paul H. Helms. (Courtesy SCCOG.)

Southern California Committee chairman Paul Helms stated Los Angeles's case for the 1952 Games to the IOC. With him, from left to right, were Mayor Fletcher Bowron, Ralph Chick, and Frank Bull. The IOC awarded the Games to Helsinki. Los Angeles tried for 1956, too, but Melbourne won. (Courtesy SCCOG.)

Between bids, the Southern California Committee worked steadily to raise funds for the US Olympic team. The American team remains unique in having no government funding. (Courtesy SCCOG.)

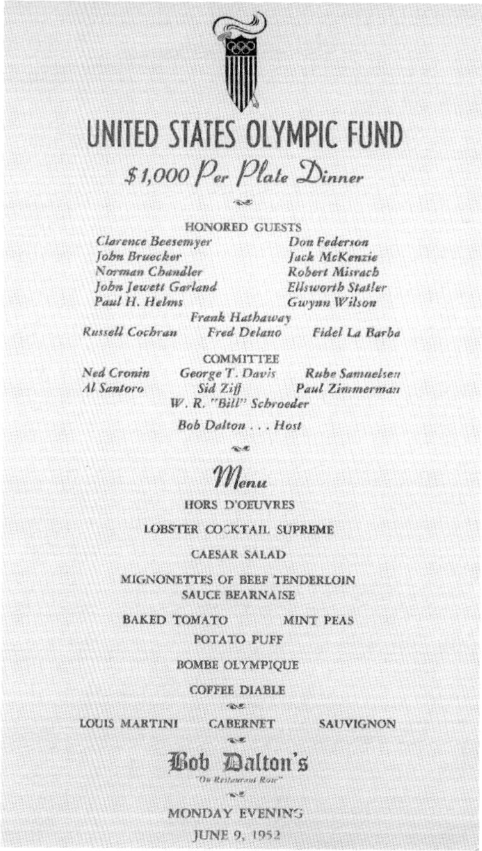

UNITED STATES OLYMPIC FUND

$1,000 Per Plate Dinner

HONORED GUESTS

Clarence Beesemyer — *Don Federson*
John Bruecker — *Jack McKenzie*
Norman Chandler — *Robert Misrach*
John Jewett Garland — *Ellsworth Statler*
Paul H. Helms — *Gwynn Wilson*
Frank Hathaway
Russell Cochran — *Fred Delano* — *Fidel La Barba*

COMMITTEE

Ned Cronin — *George T. Davis* — *Rube Samuelsen*
Al Santoro — *Sid Ziff* — *Paul Zimmerman*
W. R. "Bill" Schroeder

Bob Dalton . . . Host

Menu

HORS D'OEUVRES

LOBSTER COCKTAIL SUPREME

CAESAR SALAD

MIGNONETTES OF BEEF TENDERLOIN
SAUCE BEARNAISE

BAKED TOMATO — MINT PEAS
POTATO PUFF

BOMBE OLYMPIQUE

COFFEE DIABLE

LOUIS MARTINI — CABERNET — SAUVIGNON

Bob Dalton's
"On Restaurant Row"

MONDAY EVENING
JUNE 9, 1952

Fundraising for the team included this 1952 $1,000-per-plate dinner. In today's climate, it would be unlikely to include "Bombe Olympique" on an Olympic menu. (Courtesy SCCOG.)

Even youngsters and local beauty queens were enlisted in the fundraising efforts throughout the 1950s and 1960s. (Courtesy SCCOG.)

From 1941 to 1969, the Southern California Committee hosted the Coliseum Relays track meet at the Coliseum. It continued as the Compton Relays until 1972. Here the 1959 organizers are gathered. (Courtesy SCCOG.)

The Southern California Committee was instrumental in bringing the Olympic Winter Games to Squaw Valley, California, in 1960, and encouraged IOC members visit the Los Angeles area as well. Here Southern California Committee leader (and honorary president of the Squaw Valley Games) John Jewett Garland takes fellow IOC members on a tour of Disneyland in February 1960. Garland also led Los Angeles's bid to the USOC for the 1976 Games. (Courtesy SCCOG.)

In September 1964, as the American athletes traveled to Los Angeles en route to the Tokyo Games, Los Angeles established a Welcome Committee that provided bus transportation, a football game at the Coliseum, a visit to Disneyland, and a banquet with Mayor Sam Yorty. From left to right are Coliseum general manager William Nicholas with committee members James Kelley and Hilmer Lodge. (Courtesy SCCOG.)

Tom Bradley, Los Angeles's mayor from 1973 to 1993, picked up the Olympic baton from his predecessor, Sam Yorty, who had led an abortive run in 1969 as the American candidate city for the 1976 Games. Those Games went to Montreal. Bradley teamed with the Southern California Committee's John Argue to make a bid for the 1980 Games. When Moscow was selected, he redoubled his efforts toward 1984. (Photograph by Elisa Leonelli.)

Los Angeles's team traveled to Athens in May 1978 to present its bid for the 1984 Games to the IOC. It was the only bid the IOC received, and Los Angeles was conditionally chosen. From left to right are USOC executive director Col. F. Donald Miller and Pres. Robert Kane; Mayor Tom Bradley; IOC president Lord Killanin; Southern California Committee chair John Argue; Los Angeles chief administrative officer Anton Calleia; and city council president John Ferraro. (Courtesy SCCOG.)

John C. Argue, chair of the Southern California Committee from 1972 to 2002, led the bid effort for Los Angeles. The bid proposed private-sector financing and no government guarantees, despite contrary IOC requirements. After attempts to reach a final agreement with the IOC failed in summer 1978, Argue joined with six other private-sector representatives in a new negotiating committee that called itself the Los Angeles Olympic Organizing Committee (LAOOC). That "blue ribbon committee" pursued the negotiations to success in October 1978. Later, Argue was bestowed the IOC's highest honor, the Olympic Order (as was Peter V. Ueberroth). (Courtesy SCCOG.)

On October 20, 1978, at the White House, Mayor Bradley and IOC president Killanin signed the host city agreement under the gaze of John Argue of the Southern California Committee and Don Miller of the USOC. A final contract with the IOC was signed on March 1, 1979, in Lausanne, Switzerland. (Courtesy SCCOG.)

On October 21, 1978, LAOOC returned home to a jubilant community and a victory lunch at the Los Angeles Athletic Club. LAOOC members present at the lunch were (sitting) John Argue (fourth from left); (standing) Rodney Rood (fifth from left); William Robertson (ninth from left); and David Wolper (tenth from left). The remaining members, Howard Allen, Justin Dart, and Paul Ziffren were absent. LAOOC then restructured and expanded in order to organize the Games. (Courtesy SCCCOG.)

2

The Organizing Committee Prepares

The success of the 1984 Games was due mainly to the disciplined planning and preparation of LAOOC. A large, diverse governing board chose a young dynamic leader who assembled an enthusiastic team of volunteers and employees to execute a plan that minimized costs without lessening the experience of the Games for the IOC, the athletes, or the audience. Planning for the operations of the venues, three athletes' villages, security, transportation, ticketing, accreditation of participants and press, protocol, ceremonies, a torch relay, an arts festival, and professional and volunteer staffing make the Olympic Games a gargantuan management challenge. All the multifarious tasks had to be done under a tight time schedule. Since LAOOC was a private company with no physical assets, it had to negotiate for everything it would use, from the Coliseum to the balloons. A key to success was aggressively negotiated agreements with its business partners. Also, by keeping a tight lid on staffing until the last year before the Games, by accelerating and increasing the revenue from television and sponsorships over prior levels, by avoiding the need to build more than three venues, and by consistent cost-conscious management, the Games were able to yield surplus revenues of over $232 million for the USOC and youth sports. The absence of the ability to fall back on the taxpayers to fund overruns focused the efforts of the management in a way that would have been advantageous to other Olympic Games before and after 1984.

Despite strict controls on costs, Los Angeles expanded the scope of its ambition in important ways. Los Angeles developed new programs to engage its most prominent citizens as "commissioners" of each sport, a legion of over 33,000 additional volunteers, and its unique wealth of Southern California Olympians in the planning and public outreach for the Games. LAOOC also carried out the pre-Games obligations of a host city such as hosting IOC Executive Board meetings in 1982 and 1983 and pre-Olympic sports events in 1983. By avoiding new construction, management was able to pay attention to how the Games would be experienced by its participants and viewers. In its preparation, it built a high level of excitement and anticipation. As the Opening Ceremony approached, Los Angeles was ready.

After the IOC contract was signed, LAOOC expanded its board to 59 diverse members with John Argue as its initial chairman. It conducted a nationwide search for its chief executive. In March 1979, the board elected Paul Ziffren as its permanent chairman and Peter Ueberroth as its president. Ziffren was a distinguished Los Angeles attorney with active involvement in local and national politics and philanthropies. Ueberroth (left), a former water polo player, was an extraordinarily successful travel industry executive based in Los Angeles. His leadership of the Games is widely credited with their success. He was recognized at the end of the Games with the IOC's Olympic Order and by Time magazine as its Man of the Year. Ueberroth went on to serve as commissioner of Major League Baseball and as chairman of the USOC in addition to his business endeavors. Though LAOOC was a private-sector organization, Ueberroth maintained a very close working relationship with Mayor Bradley, shown below meeting with him at the original LAOOC offices on Santa Monica Boulevard in Century City.

Olympic finances were transformed forever in a single stroke in September 1979 by the $225-million US television rights deal being signed above by, from left to right, Charles Stanford and John Martin of ABC Sports, Peter Ueberroth, and Lord Killanin and Monique Berlioux of the IOC. It was the highest television rights fee ever paid for any event and almost triple the amount paid for the prior Games in Moscow. Advance payments under the contract financed LAOOC operations for years.

Prominent attorney and Peter Ueberroth confidant Harry Usher joined LAOOC as executive vice president and general manager on February 1, 1980. The ABC television agreement and the initial sponsorship agreements had been entered, but almost all other planning and operations remained to be done. Usher oversaw all operations of the organization and is credited with much of its success. After the Games, he was commissioner of the United States Football League, which operated until 1987.

On August 4, 1980, LAOOC chairman Paul Ziffren and Mayor Tom Bradley unveiled the "Star in Motion" emblem of the Games. Designed by Robert Miles Runyon and Associates, it was rendered in red, white, and blue and became the ubiquitous symbol of the Games, promoted all over the world by LAOOC, its sponsors, suppliers, and broadcasters.

Mascots had been a feature of the Games since the Munich 1972 Games. The 1984 mascot, "Sam the Olympic Eagle," was created by C. Robert Moore of Walt Disney Productions. It was used extensively at youth events leading up to the Games and was a cherished image on souvenirs.

In 1980, long before the Soviet boycott, Marat Gramov, chairman of the USSR Sports Committee and National Olympic Committee, and Peter Ueberroth signed a protocol agreement at the offices of LAOOC, then located in the UCLA Extension Building.

From 1982 to 1983, LAOOC occupied an office building it built on a UCLA parking lot on LeConte Avenue in Westwood. It is now UCLA's Peter V. Ueberroth Olympic Office Building. (Photograph by author.)

Television rights sales for broadcast outside the United States totaled about $60 million, which was more than quadruple the total such fees at the prior Games. Michael O'Hara, LAOOC vice president/television, led the effort. Above, in April 1983, from left to right, the author and O'Hara for LAOOC and Oscar Gutierrez and Amaury Daumas for Organización de Televisión Iberoamericana (OTI) conclude an agreement for Latin American television rights stipulating an unprecedented fee of over $2 million.

As Games preparations progressed, Peter Ueberroth toured IOC president Juan Antonio Samaranch and IOC director Monique Berlioux through the Coliseum.

Planning for ticket sales by an internal LAOOC ticketing department led by vice president/ticketing G. Edward Smith began in 1981, and order taking commenced in May 1983. Over 83 percent of all available tickets were sold. Most of the key events were sold out. Prices for competition events ranged from $3 to $95, with an average ticket price of $17. Several events were unticketed and free to the public. Over three million tickets were offered at $10 or less.

In April 1981, Peter Ueberroth, accompanied by LAOOC vice president Joel Rubenstein and LAOOC's Japan representative Jimmy Fukuzaki of the advertising firm Dentsu, Inc. (center), entered the first LAOOC Official Supplier agreement with Brother Industries, Ltd., of Japan for the supply of typewriters. Rubenstein and LAOOC vice president/corporate relations Daniel Greenwood led the sponsorship and licensing campaign.

Beginning with the Tokyo 1964 Games, pictograms have been a feature of the Olympic Games, particularly for use with directional signage. They allow easy communication across linguistic and cultural lines. LAOOC introduced these 23 pictograms designed in 1981 by Keith Bright and Associates.

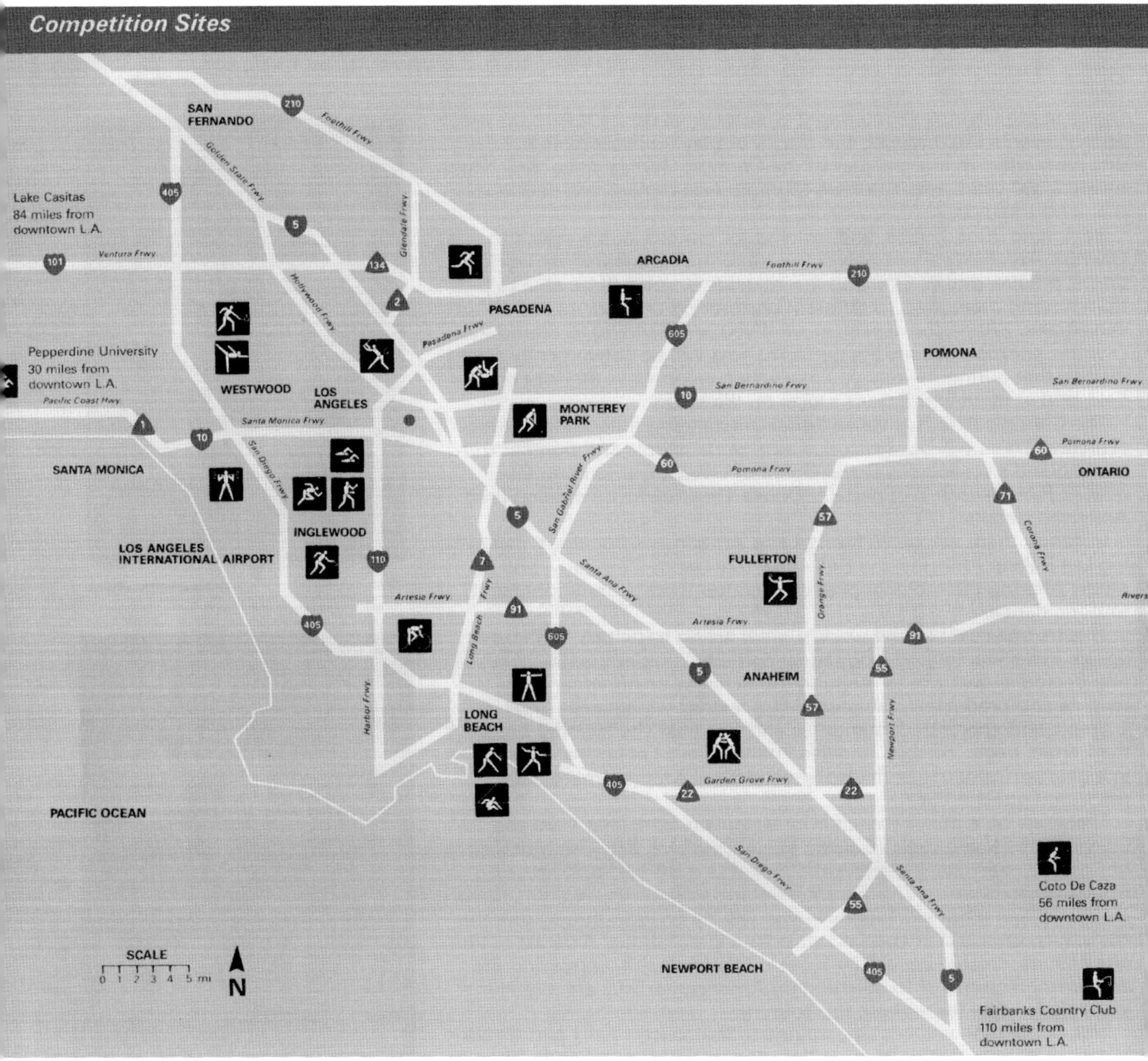

This abstract map of the Los Angeles area with its freeway grid shows the breadth of the Games, with venues located from Santa Barbara to San Diego Counties.

Competition at the Olympic Games is not limited to the field of play. Pin trading among the fans is a time-honored Olympic tradition, and the left pins developed by LAOOC are only a sampling of those available in 1984.

The California Legislature and Department of Motor Vehicles joined in doing things new and differently by issuing in honor of the Games the state's first commemorative license plates. A portion of the revenue went to LAOOC's charitable purposes. It began a practice in the state of supporting valuable causes with personalized license plate sales.

The open plan of the final office facilities of LAOOC facilitated free communication and staff growth. These offices filled a 180,000-square-foot former Hughes Helicopter design and engineering facility at Lincoln and Washington Boulevards near Marina del Rey. From January 1983 to May 1984, LAOOC staff grew from less than 200 to 1,750 personnel.

In 1983, a series of pre-Olympic events were held as part of LAOOC's preparations for the Games. The World Target Archery Championships were held at the Olympic venue, El Dorado Park in Long Beach. Other pre-Olympic events occurred in cycling, diving, gymnastics, rowing, swimming, and synchronized swimming. A pre-Olympic shooting event occurred in 1984. (Photograph by Elisa Leonelli.)

LAOOC's outreach to the public included an innovative "Spirit Team" composed of Olympians who performed public speeches and appearances before all kinds of audiences in Southern California and elsewhere to build knowledge of and anticipation for the Games. There are more Olympians in Southern California than anywhere else in the world. The team began with 84 local Olympians in March 1983 and swelled to 250 by 1984.

With the athletes, press, guests, volunteers, and staff numbering over 100,000, and security as a significant concern, accreditation required major effort by LAOOC. Each eligible person was issued a badge such as that at left, which bore a series of codes and identifying markings that signified the holder's category and access privileges. It was supported by state-of-the-art computer technology and readable by bar code readers.

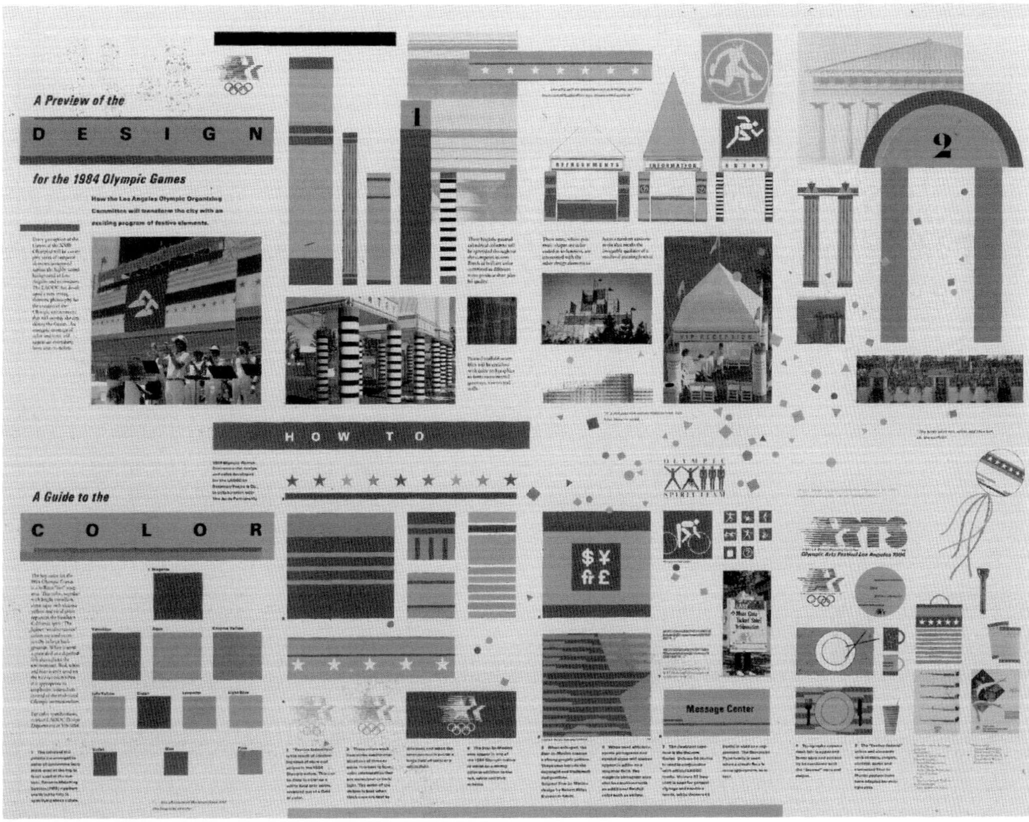

The "look" of the Games was unveiled in February 1984. Created by designer Deborah Sussman and architect Jon Jerde, it combined pastel colors called "Festive Federalism" with bright, friendly, modular, temporary constructions that enabled a transformation of diverse existing venues and other sites across the city into distinctive, recognizable, celebratory locales. It avoided nationalism and embraced friendliness and a party atmosphere. Its components, shown above, are also shown in use at the weightlifting venue below.

The success of the Games, financially and in their smooth operation, owed much to the use of Los Angeles's wealth of existing facilities of Olympic quality. Still, an Olympic pool, a shooting range, and a cycling venue were needed. Beyond that, the only construction requirements for the Games were some venue renovations, a dining hall, and temporary office and venue facilities for the special needs of the Games. With a donation from McDonald's Corporation, LAOOC built the Olympic Swim Stadium at the University of Southern California (shown under construction above and completed below) to accommodate swimming and diving. It remains in use. (Above, photograph by Elisa Leonelli.)

With a donation from Southland Corporation (7-11 Stores), LAOOC built an outdoor velodrome at California State University Dominguez Hills for cycling events. The velodrome (shown under construction above and completed below) was replaced in 2003 with an indoor velodrome, the ADT Events Center, as part of a larger multisport complex. A shooting range was built for the Games at the Prado Recreation Area in Chino, California. (Above, photograph by Elisa Leonelli.)

More than 10,000 athletes and officials were housed in existing residence halls converted to Athletes' Villages at the University of Southern California (USC) (above), UCLA, and UC Santa Barbara. The Villages featured food halls, sports training facilities and equipment, and entertainment areas, as well as all other amenities suitable to the athletes' needs. These were the first Olympic Games in which the women and men were housed in the same buildings.

Since the terrorism of the Munich 1972 Games, security has been a major concern of Olympic organizers. Among LAOOC's extensive precautions were scans above and below each bus that transported athletes from the Athletes' Villages to the venues. Thorough security planning headed by LAOOC vice president Edgar Best in coordination with dozens of local and federal law enforcement agencies resulted in the absence of any major incidents at the Games. The Games were a breakthrough in cooperation among police agencies. The services of over 18,000 private and public security personnel were paid for by LAOOC.

The "look" of the Games was applied throughout the Athletes' Villages, as here on the "Main Street" promenade created at the Village at USC.

Pictograms and the "look" combined to decorate and identify the archery venue at El Dorado Park in Long Beach.

LAOOC introduced radically new communications systems for the athletes. This IBM Olympic Message System offered an innovation called voice mail, and the AT&T Electronic Messaging System (EMS) was an early version of e-mail. Through both systems, the athletes tasted the future in communicating with family, friends, journalists, and other competitors. The EMS carried about three million messages during the Games.

More than 33,000 uniforms in polyester bearing the pastels of "Festive Federalism" were specially designed and manufactured by Games sponsor Levi Strauss & Company for LAOOC employees and volunteers. Each person was fitted at one of several large distribution centers in June 1984. The uniforms, in 11 styles, contributed to the "look" of the Games and gave the personnel a consistent and identifiable appearance to the audience.

The 330,000-square-foot Los Angeles Convention Center at Twelfth and Figueroa Streets (above) was converted to be the Olympic Press Center. It opened on July 5, 1984, and served thousands of journalists and photographers from around the world. The center's facilities, such as the technology center shown below, were used by over 3,800 writers, photographers, and technicians and were under the direction of LAOOC vice president Richard Perelman.

As the Games approached in the summer of 1984, all of Los Angeles put on its party clothes. The Los Angeles Federal Savings tower in North Hollywood was covered in an Olympic mural, as were many buildings across town. (Photograph by Elisa Leonelli.)

Each Olympic Games designs its own medals. The reverse of the 1984 medals is shown right.

3

The Olympic Arts Festival and the Torch Relay Set the Stage

Since the Stockholm 1912 Games there have been cultural events associated with the Games as required by the Olympic Charter. Some were modest affairs tangential to the sporting events. LAOOC created an unprecedented program of broad local and international participation that was central to its mission. In its 10-week Olympic Arts Festival, LAOOC gathered 37 local arts organizations as coproducers of 432 performances of dance, music, and theater at 21 sites, as well as 31 visual arts commissions, exhibitions, and events at 26 sites. Seventy-five performing arts companies came from 18 countries. The total ticketed attendance for the festival was over 1.25 million people, and many festival programs could be enjoyed without a ticket. The festival opened the Games to the public while building community interest to a fever pitch.

There were many American debuts, including Germany's Wuppertaler Tanztheater, Australia's Circus Oz, and Great Britain's Royal Opera of Covent Garden. Forty-five impressionist masterpieces from the Louvre were shipped to Los Angeles. The Kasuga Shrine in Japan loaned the festival ancient ceremonial masks and robes that had not previously been seen outside the shrine in Nara.

The other antecedent to the Games was the torch relay. Commencing with the Berlin 1936 Games, there have been torch relays from Olympia, Greece, to the sites of each of the Games, but there had never been a relay like this one. The relay began on May 8 in New York and ended 82 days later at the Opening Ceremony. It passed through 33 states, the longest Olympic relay to that date. It had been intended to reach all 50 states, but the start was delayed and the number of runners limited by the reluctance of Greek officials to agree to turn over the Olympic Flame for a relay sponsored by a private company and seeking to raise donations for youth sports charities. They decried these LAOOC innovations as "commercialism." After much negotiation, led by LAOOC vice president Richard Sargent, Greece did provide the flame in a private ceremony at Olympia. As the flame passed from runner to runner across the United States, it ignited a nationwide passion for the upcoming Games. Moreover, almost $11 million was raised for worthy charities.

The Olympic Arts Festival featured 432 performances by 146 theater, dance, and music companies representing every continent and 19 countries. Le Théâtre du Soleil (left), a Parisian avant-garde stage ensemble founded by Ariane Mnouchkine, made its maiden American appearance at the festival with performances of *Shakespeare's Henry IV, Part 1; Richard II* (below); and *Twelfth Night* at Television Center in Hollywood, Studio 9.

Robert Fitzpatrick (left), pictured with sculptor Robert Graham (right), directed the Olympic Arts Festival, assisted by associate directors Hope Tschopik and Peter Schneider. Fitzpatrick concurrently served as president of the California Institute of the Arts. In 1987, he founded and directed the Los Angeles Arts Festival, which grew out of the Olympic Arts Festival. Thereafter, he headed Euro Disney Resort near Paris, the school of art of Columbia University, and the Museum of Contemporary Art in Chicago. (Photograph by Elisa Leonelli.)

Robert Graham created the 25-foot-tall Olympic Gateway at the entrance to the Coliseum as a legacy of the Games. Made of cast bronze, gold leaf, and zinc, it depicts emblematic female and male athletes. Two 1984 competitors posed for Graham: then-Guyanese (and later United States) long jumper Jennifer Innis and American water polo team captain Terry Schroeder (who became US Olympic water polo coach in 2008 and 2012.) The work was dedicated on June 1, 1984, as the opening event of the Olympic Arts Festival. (Photograph by Elisa Leonelli.)

Artist George Romero painted *Going to the Olympics* as part of the Olympic Arts Festival freeway mural program. Ten artists designed and executed freeway murals that lasted for years on the Santa Ana and Harbor Freeways leading to downtown Los Angeles. (Photograph by Elisa Leonelli.)

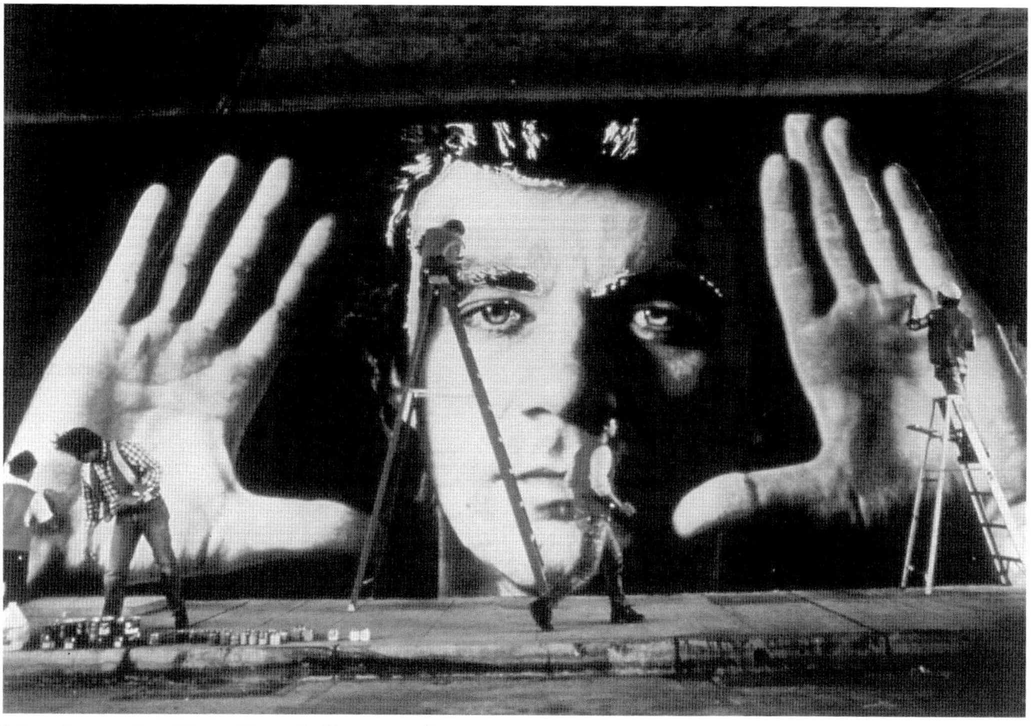

Noted muralist Kent Twitchell painted a double mural, *Seventh Street Altarpiece*, on the 110 Freeway under opposite sides of the Seventh Street overpass. This portion was called *Jim Morphesis Monument*.

The insignia of the Olympic Arts Festival, in the pastel colors of the Games, were displayed at every theater, museum, or other venue of the activities of the festival all over Southern California. The star above, with fuchsia lettering and orange background, was erected over the Fisher Gallery at USC. (Photograph by Elisa Leonelli.)

David Hockney joined 15 other fine artists in doing Olympic posters commissioned by the arts festival. Posters had always been a part of the Games, but this was the first use of a cadre of well-known painters to create serious works. Hockney's contribution, shown above, reflected his frequent use of images of Southern California's iconic swimming pools embellished by a pattern of partial Olympic rings. (Photograph by Elisa Leonelli.)

Artist Robert Rauschenberg's contribution to the Olympic poster series was a variation on the theme of LAOOC's "Star in Motion" emblem.

Though not a part of the official arts festival program, popular artist LeRoy Neiman joined in and created two Olympic-themed paintings. He posed at the Playboy Mansion in Holmby Hills with his paintings, a cigar, and a parrot. (Photograph by Elisa Leonelli.)

The Japanese dance troupe Sankai Juku brought their *butoh*-style performance to the arts festival at the Pasadena Civic Auditorium. Prior to their ticketed shows, they gave a free public performance of *Sholiba*, involving performers wearing powder suspended upside down lowering themselves from the roof of the Dorothy Chandler Pavilion of the Music Center.

While many Olympics Arts Festival events were free to the public, most had limited capacity and required tickets. Over 300,000 tickets were sold to ticketed events at an average price of $14 each for total revenue of almost $5 million.

The California Museum of Afro-American History and Culture (now known as the California African American Museum) in Exposition Park presented a show of The Black Olympians: 1904–1984. This festival show was the museum's inaugural public exhibition. Anita DeFrantz, Olympic rower in the 1976 Games in Montreal, whose display is pictured above, went on to become a member of the IOC and president of the LA84 Foundation, a legacy of the Games. (Photograph by Elisa Leonelli.)

The show at the Temporary Contemporary facility of the Museum of Contemporary Art in downtown Los Angeles was focused on the automobile in culture—an appropriate theme for Games in Los Angeles.

The ARCO Center for Visual Art in downtown Los Angeles staged an exhibition called Los Angeles and the Palm Tree: Image of a City. It highlighted the city's iconic tree, 25,000 of which were planted to beautify the city for the Los Angeles 1932 Games.

An exhibition of an international festival of masks, Masks in Motion, was held at the Craft and Folk Art Museum in the Mid-Wilshire district.

The Royal Winnipeg Ballet of Canada danced nine performances at the Pasadena Civic Auditorium.

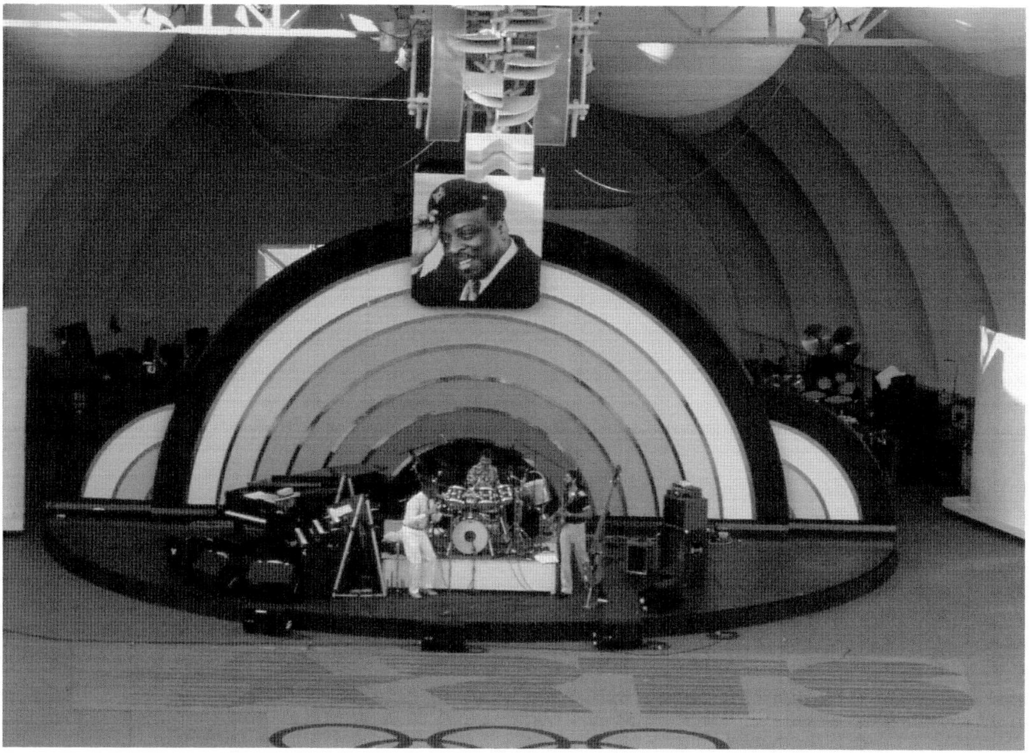

The Hollywood Bowl was the scene of the Great Olympic Jazz Marathon.

The Japan America Theater hosted eight performances before sold-out houses for the Kodo drummers of Japan.

The torch relay, bringing the Olympic flame from Olympia, Greece, to the Games, covered 15,000 kilometers across America. It was sponsored and conducted by Games sponsor AT&T. Torch relays have been a part of the Olympic Games since the Berlin 1936 Games, but this was the longest to date and the first one used to raise funds for charity.

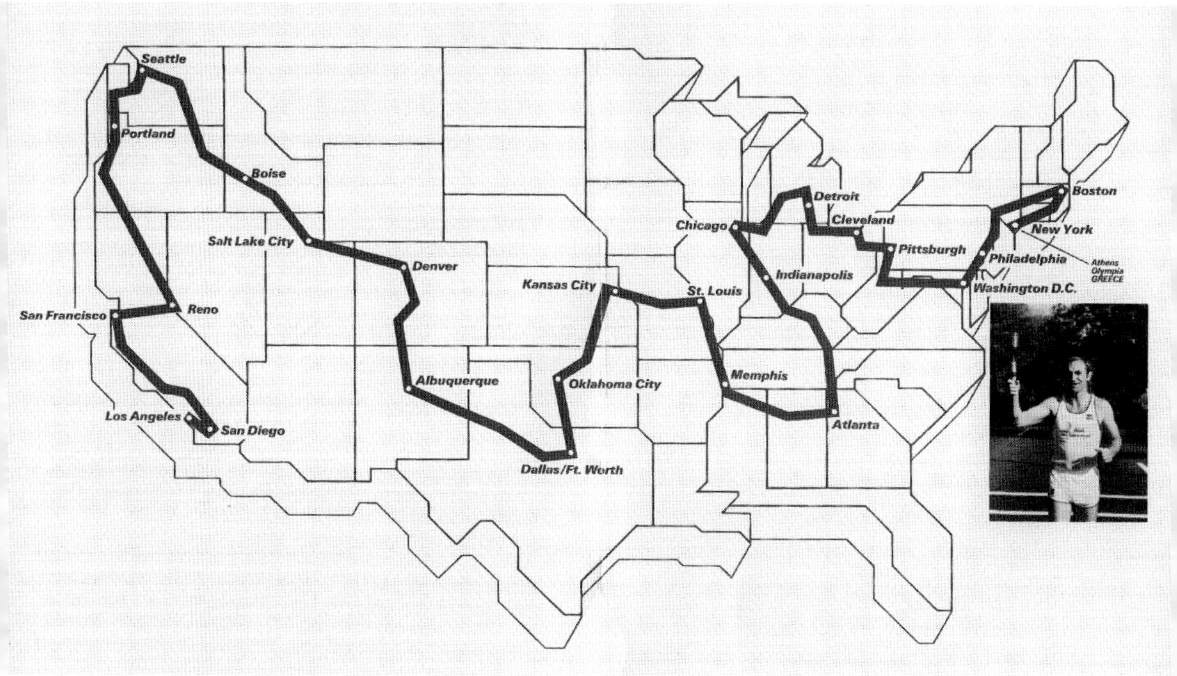

The relay route across 33 states began in New York City and ended in Los Angeles.

The relay began at United Nations Plaza in New York on a rainy May 8, 1984. The flame from Olympia had flown on a White House plane from Greece. The first two torches were lit by Rafer Johnson and handed to Bill Thorpe Jr. (left) and Gina Hemphill, grandchildren of Olympic greats Jim Thorpe and Jesse Owens, respectively. They ran the first kilometer through the streets of New York City.

The torch runners were welcomed at the White House by Pres. Ronald Reagan before heading west.

The torch was made by the official supplier to the Games, Turner Industries, Inc. It was 22 inches tall with a five-inch bowl and weighed three pounds when full of fuel. It had a leather handle over an aluminum body decorated with an antique brass finish and the Olympic motto, "*Citius, Altius, Fortius.*"

The relay was run by 3,636 runners, young and old. Anyone could participate by donating, or having donated on their behalf, $3,000 to the Torch Relay Foundation for the benefit of youth sports programs. Almost $11 million was raised and distributed, mostly to YMCA, Special Olympics, and Boys and Girls Clubs of America by donations of these Youth Legacy Kilometers.

Across the enormous breadth of the nation, carrying the torch was sometimes a solitary joy, as here in Colorado.

The relay was open to the fully abled and the disabled. People walked. People ran barefoot. People danced. They moved joyfully in whatever way worked for them. Participation was so much in demand that by the end of the relay, an extra detour toward San Diego had to be added to accommodate a portion of the outstanding requests.

Crowds greeted the torch through more than 1,000 communities. In every small town and suburb, witnesses lined the streets. In New York (above right), it drew over 700,000 people; in Chicago and Dallas over 200,000; and in Seattle over 500,000. It went through downtown Denver to ebullient crowds (left).

Finally, in Los Angeles (right), more than 2.5 million turned out. The torch relay built the entire nation's enthusiasm for the Games as a single moving pep rally.

4

THE CEREMONY OPENS THE GAMES

The Games raised the Opening Ceremony to a new standard that has been elaborated upon and enlarged but not fundamentally changed since 1984. The Opening Ceremony set the tone. Many elements of the ceremony, such as flags, torches, and marching, are dictated by the Olympic Charter and by tradition and tend to give a martial flavor more reminiscent of ancient Rome than ancient Greece. In contrast, LAOOC presented a celebratory mood, with an emphasis on harmony. Also, as the entertainment capital of the world with about 2.5 billion people watching, Los Angeles wanted to entertain as well as to impress.

Initially, LAOOC selected the Disney Company to create the ceremony. However, less than one year before the Games, when estimates for the Disney plans exceeded LAOOC's budget, LAOOC appointed television and film producer David Wolper to produce opening and closing ceremonies. Wolper had been among the original seven-member LAOOC that negotiated with the IOC to bring the Games to Los Angeles and had been key to the landmark ABC-LAOOC television agreement. He retained experienced special events expert Tommy Walker as ceremonies director.

In a change from prior Opening Ceremonies, Wolper and Walker moved the entertainment portion of the show to before the entry of the athletes so there would be room on the infield for a presentation on the scale of the Coliseum. They recruited a cast of more than 9,000 amateur marching band musicians, drill teams, and choristers from colleges and universities as well as professional dancers to put on a six-part show, *Music of America*. Its playful humor and innocence and the upbeat tunes from Sousa to Big Band put the festivities on a cheerful path to the formalities and solemnities to follow.

Perhaps the most thrilling moments of the Opening Ceremony were not scripted. When the Romanian team, which had defied the Soviet boycott, entered the Coliseum, everyone rose and cheered in unison to salute its bravery. The big team from the People's Republic of China got a similarly warm welcome to its first Olympic Games.

The evening ended with a young unknown singer, Vicki McClure, singing "Reach Out and Touch" as every person present, audience, officials, and athletes, joined hands and sang with her. The obligatory but spectacular fireworks ensued.

Ceremony executive producer and commissioner David Wolper was a producer who had made over 300 films and television shows and won over 150 awards, including Oscars, Emmys, Golden Globes, and Peabodys. His introduction to the Olympic Games had been his production of the official film of the Munich 1972 Games, *Visions of Eight*. He served as vice chairman of the LAOOC and later as chairman of the LA84 Foundation.

As the Coliseum filled for the Opening Ceremony, the infield contained performers holding over 1,200 five-foot diameter helium-filled balloons. Each of the 92,655 spectators held a "Welcome" flag given out on entrance to the stadium.

As church bells rang all across Los Angeles and a countdown by the crowd reached "zero," 110 trumpeters and 20 timpanists played the new *Olympic Fanfare* composed by John Williams. It has since become a staple of the American Olympic movement.

To the astonishment of the audience, "Rocket Man" William Suitor flew into the stadium propelled by a Bell Aerosystems rocket pack and landed on the field. "That thing literally exploded off that stage. I have never had it take off like that in my life," Suitor recalled.

Then, accompanied by "Welcome," an original song by composer Marvin Hamlisch and lyricist Dean Pitchford, the helium balloons were released, each trailing a streamer reading "Welcome" in one of 23 languages.

Following the release of the balloons, Pres. Ronald Reagan, IOC president Juan Antonio Samaranch, and LAOOC president Peter Ueberroth were introduced, the flag of the United States was presented and raised, and the national anthem of the United States was sung by jazz singer Etta James accompanied by a 60-piece Olympic orchestra and 1,000-member Olympic choir placed at the peristyle end of the Coliseum.

The 800-person All-American Olympic marching band entered the stadium. The band consisted of 144 trumpets, 96 trombones, 48 sousaphones, 48 percussion instruments, 64 piccolos and flutes, 52 clarinets, and 108 saxophones, all drawn from collegiate bands.

The band was joined by 1,262 members of the Olympic Drill Team.

The drill team formed up the outline of the United States as an introduction to a six-part, 30-minute show called *Music of America*, presenting thousands of costumed performers in the infield.

Following a segment of marches by the band, called "Americana Suite," a segment called "Pioneer Spirit" celebrated the American westward movement of the 19th century.

The performers included 300 members of the Olympic dance corps, 50 youth dancers, 50 gymnasts/fiddlers, and 10 character dancers.

"Pioneer Spirit" had everything from Conestoga wagons to movable props that set up a frontier town in the infield.

In a segment titled "Dixieland Jamboree," the band was joined by 300 gospel singers from local churches and 75 dancers to perform jazz and gospel music. The culmination was Etta James's rendition of "When the Saints Go Marching In" in front of a cloth set made to look like stained-glass windows.

"Urban Rhapsody" melded the jazz and classical influences of American music by a performance of George Gershwin's *Rhapsody in Blue* on 84 black pianos and one white piano accompanied by 200 dancers. The last segments celebrated Big Band music of the 1930s and 1940s and invited the entire cast of over 9,000 performers onto the field for the finale in the shape of the United States.

Following the musical entertainment portion of the program, the entire audience except the working press participated in the largest card stunt in Olympic history—85,000 cards represented the flags of every one of the 140 nations at the Games.

Then the official proceedings began. As required by the Olympic Charter, Louis Guirandou N'Diaye, IOC first vice president and member from the Ivory Coast, carried the original Olympic flag, the flag first flown at the 1920 Antwerp Games, into the Coliseum and presented it to IOC president Samaranch, who handed it to Mayor Bradley, who waved it and then passed it to LAOOC chairman Ziffren and then to LAOOC executive vice president Usher.

Composer John Williams stepped to the podium to lead the orchestra in the Coliseum in his new Olympic theme music that extended and elaborated the fanfare that had been heard earlier. The music was accompanied in the infield by the choreography of hundreds of "silks"—performers clad in white bearing white and gold Olympic pennants.

The March of the Athletes began with the entrance of Greece, an honor that was traditionally given to the Greeks in recognition of their ancient Olympic games. LAOOC had threatened to withhold this honor if Greece had held to its refusal to provide the Olympic flame for the torch relay.

The Japanese team marches with red jackets and white hats.

The entrance of the delegation of 213 from China, in defiance of the Soviet boycott, brought the entire crowd to its feet in appreciation. It was the People's Republic of China's first Olympic Games.

The Jordanians marched in native dress.

As the hosts, the team from the United States marched in last. Hammer thrower Ed Burke, the oldest member of the team at age 44, was the flag bearer leading the delegation of 589.

As each team circled the field on the track, it passed the peristyle with its name and flag displayed on the electronic screens.

After circling the field, the teams formed in the infield behind their plaques. A record-setting 140 national Olympic committee teams participated. The March of the Athletes took one hour and 22 minutes.

LAOOC president Ueberroth and IOC president Samaranch (foreground) addressed the athletes and audience. Samaranch closed his remarks with "God Bless America" and invited the president of the United States to proclaim the Games open.

President and Mrs. Reagan occupied the press box above the stadium. President Reagan stated, "Celebrating the XXIIIrd Olympiad of the modern era, I declare open the Olympic Games of Los Angeles." It marked the first time a sitting American president opened an Olympic Games.

The entrance of the Olympic flag to fly over the Coliseum throughout the Games was entrusted to 11 men and women who were American Olympic legends: Bruce Jenner, Sammy Lee, Pat McCormick, Billy Mills, John Naber, Parry O'Brien, Al Oerter, Mack Robinson, Richard Sandoval, Bill Thorpe Jr., and Wyomia Tyus.

The march of the Olympic flag to the peristyle flagpole and the raising of the flag were accompanied by the 1,100-member Olympic choir singing the "Olympic Hymn," composed for the Athens 1896 Games by Spyros Samaras and translated to English with amended lyrics for the 1984 Games by Earl Brown. As the flag reached the top of the pole, 4,000 homing pigeons were released from the Coliseum field to symbolize peace.

As the original composition *The Olympian* by the famed composer Philip Glass was played, Gina Hemphill emerged from the tunnel into the stadium with the Olympic torch. She had run the first kilometer of the torch relay along with Bill Thorpe Jr., and now she ran the last.

Hemphill did one lap of the track and handed the torch to the final runner, Rafer Johnson, the great decathlon champion of the Rome 1960 Olympic Games. He had lit the first torch in New York City. Johnson began his run around the track toward the peristyle and the cauldron.

After climbing 96 steps (including many at a breathless 50 degree angle), Johnson paused dramatically. Then he touched the torch to a tube filled with natural gas and lit the Olympic Rings, which in turn lit the cauldron that was to remain ablaze for the duration of the Games.

Then the flags of the 140 participating teams were paraded around the stadium to form a semicircle around the speakers' podium, whereupon American team member Edwin Moses, who had won a gold medal in the 400-meter hurdles at the Montreal 1976 Games, took the athlete's oath on behalf of all the competitors, and Sharon Weber, American gymnastics official, took the official's oath on behalf of all the judges and officials.

As the flags returned to their positions, 2,000 volunteers from worldwide backgrounds in native dress surrounded the athletes on the track, and an international children's choir sang the "Ode to Joy" from Beethoven's Ninth Symphony.

Vicki McClure, a singer chosen from the chorus, emerged to sing "Reach Out and Touch." As the words scrolled across one screen and videos of people around the world singing were displayed on the other screen, all the athletes and audience spontaneously joined hands and sang. The sky filled with fireworks.

5

THE ATHLETES COMPETE

Competitions proceeded from July 29 to August 12 in beautiful, pleasant weather under pollution-free skies: an average high in downtown Los Angeles of 83.7 degrees (28.7 Celsius) and no day warmer than 87 degrees (30.5 Celsius). Los Angeles's storied traffic congestion took a holiday, enabling record crowds to attend the events spread all over the region. Crime virtually ceased. Los Angeles was celebrating.

The Los Angeles 1984 Games introduced a number of new sports and disciplines to expand and diversify the Olympic Games, especially for women. It added to the card for women in athletics (track and field) a marathon, a 3,000-meter race, and a 400-meter hurdles event. The women's pentathlon grew to a heptathlon by including a 200-meter race and a javelin throw. Synchronized swimming, rhythmic gymnastics, and wind surfing made their first Olympic appearances. In shooting, women began to compete in pistol and standard rifle disciplines, and men and women commenced air rifle contests. The boxers added a super heavyweight category. As demonstration sports (an Olympic practice since discontinued), Dodger Stadium hosted a baseball competition and UCLA was the site of a tennis tournament.

The Games featured an abundance of thrilling and record-breaking performances. The United States led the medal count with 83 gold medals and a total of 174 medals. Romania won 20 gold medals, and West Germany (Federal Republic of Germany) was third with 17 gold medals. The Soviet boycott did diminish the level of competition in some sports, such as weightlifting, in which all 10 of the reigning world champions were absent. Nevertheless, the Games yielded 12 new world records (and one tie) and 81 new Olympic records (plus nine ties). For the United States, it was almost a medal overload. The USOC took the whole team on a post-Games nationwide tour of six cities, with ticker-tape parades and adoring throngs lining the streets. It ended at the White House, where President Reagan feted the athletes.

While the afterglow of the Opening Ceremony lingered, the competitions of the Games began with a bang the next morning at 8:00 on Sunday, July 29.

The Soviet bloc boycott did not detract from the fun. Only 13 nations followed the lead of the Soviets by staying home. Boycotts for one or another cause had been a perennial feature of the Games starting in 1956, but they had little effect in advancing the causes for which they were declared. Since 1984, there have been virtually no boycotts.

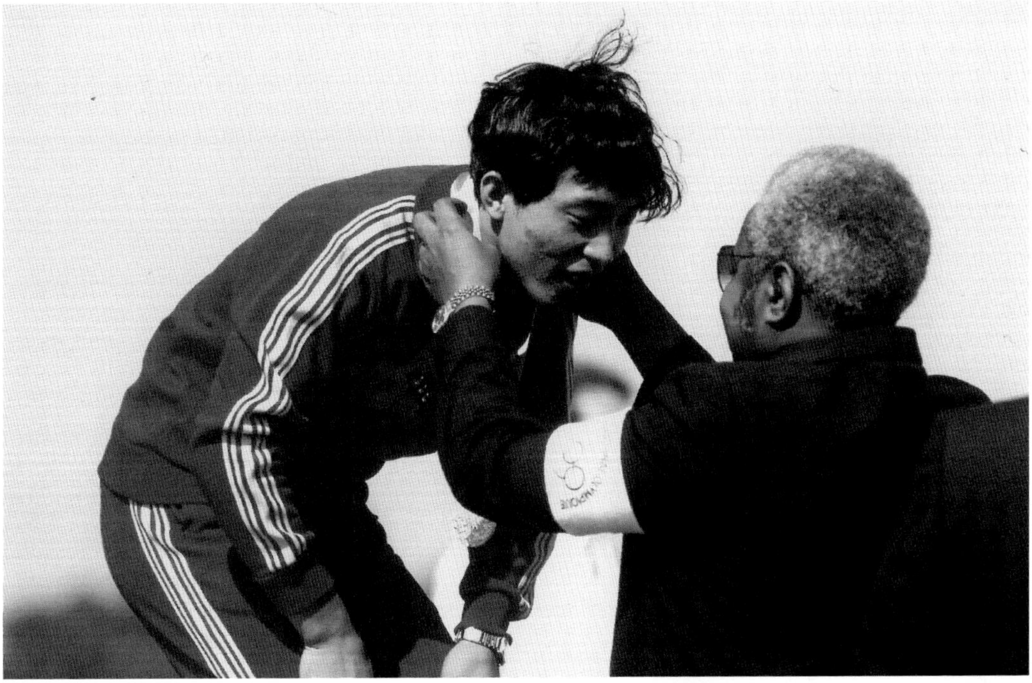

The People's Republic of China in its maiden appearance in Olympic competition captured the first gold medal when Xu Haifeng won the 50-meter free pistol competition.

This was the first Olympic medal in history for China and a harbinger of China's Olympic eminence in years to come. (Photograph by Skeeter Hagler, courtesy of NOPP/*LA Times*.)

The silver medal for 75-kilogram weightlifting went to Jacques Demers of Canada (left). Karl-Heinz Radschinsky of Germany won the gold.

Nepalese weightlifter Surenda Hamal (right) competed in the 67.5-kilogram category. The event was won by Yao Jingyuan of China.

German Michael Gross set world records in winning the 200-meter freestyle (1:47.44) and 100-meter butterfly (53.08). He also took silver in the 200-meter butterfly and 4x200-meter freestyle. Called "the Albatross" for the wingspan of his arms at 2.13 meters (seven feet), he entered the Games as a favorite. In the 4x200-meter freestyle, he swam the fastest relay leg in the event's history, but the American team pulled an upset and was dubbed the "Grossbusters."

Los Angeles pioneered the massive use of volunteers to stage the Games. It has been imitated in every Olympic Games since 1984. Some 33,000 volunteers did all kinds of tasks, from ushering to driving to translating to top administrative duties. They wore distinctive uniforms in the pale pastels of "Festive Federalism." Here are volunteers Andrew Knox, venue director of swimming, and Mary Jo Swalley (left) along with an unidentified colleague at the Olympic pool at USC.

Alex Baumann of Canada celebrated his double gold medal victories in the 200-meter and 400-meter individual medleys. Both victories set world records. The 400-meter win was Canada's first gold medal in swimming since 1912. In 2009, swimming in the 45–49 age bracket in a masters competition, he set the world record for the 200-meter medley by over three seconds.

Richard Carey of the United States won the gold medal in the 200-meter backstroke in an Olympic record time of 2:00.23. David Wilson of the United States and Mike West of Canada took silver and bronze, respectively.

Victor Davis of Canada set a world record of 2:13.34 in winning gold in the 200-meter breaststroke. Davis won silver in the 100-meter breaststroke and the 4x100-meter medley relay. In 1989, shortly after retiring from swimming, he was tragically struck by a car and died at age 25.

The United States dominated the relays, winning all three in world record times: the medley at 3:39.90; the 4x100-meter at 3:19.03; and the 4x200-meter at 7:15.69. The 4x100-meter confirmed the American leadership in this event—the only active Olympic event that the United States had always won. But most exciting was the 4x200-meter relay with Bruce Hayes's final lap victory over Germany's Michael Gross by a margin of .04 seconds.

A total of about 386,000 people attended the eight baseball games at Dodger Stadium. On the basis of the success of baseball at the Los Angeles Games, baseball was added to the Olympic program beginning at Barcelona in 1992 and continuing through the Beijing Games in 2008.

The bronze medal in the exhibition baseball tournament at Dodger Stadium went to Chinese Taipei (above), which competed separately from the People's Republic of China. Japan beat the United States for the gold medal.

Wrestling was held at the Anaheim Convention Center. Super heavyweight Jeff Blatnick, who had overcome life-threatening cancer two years earlier, won the first gold medal in American history in Greco-Roman wrestling. His teammates chose him to carry the American flag at the Closing Ceremony.

Randy Lewis of the United States won the gold medal in freestyle wrestling, 62-kilogram division. Here he defeated Cris Brown of Australia.

Men's hockey, contested at East Los Angeles College, yielded gold, silver, and bronze to Pakistan, Germany, and Great Britain, respectively. Above, Australia defeated the United States 2-1.

Karch Kiraly led an American men's volleyball team to a gold medal, the nation's first Olympic medal in the history of the event. In 1996, Kiraly became the only person to win Olympic medals in both indoor and beach volleyball. All were gold medals.

Italy, France, Germany, and Romania dominated the medal stands at the Long Beach Convention Center in the fencing competition.

Jujie Luan from China (left) and Cornelia Hanisch from Germany battled for gold in women's foil in fencing. Luan took the top medal. (Photograph by Ken Hively, courtesy of NOPP/*LA Times*.)

In the women's team foil competition in fencing, Susan Badders of the United States (left) faced Huahua Li of China. Germany, Romania, and France took the gold, silver, and bronze medals, respectively. (Photograph by Pat Downs, courtesy of NOPP/*LA Times*.)

Gymnast Mitch Gaylord led the American team to its upset win over reigning world champion China with a perfect 10 on rings—the first by any American gymnast in Olympic competition. The other team members were Bart Conner, Tim Daggett, Jim Hartung, Scott Johnson, Jim Mikus, and Peter Vidmar. This remains the only Olympic team gold medal in United States men's gymnastics history. Gaylord won four medals at the Games.

China's star gymnast Li Ning won six medals, including golds for rings, pommel horse, and floor exercise. He was China's most successful athlete at the Games. After retiring from competition, he founded the very successful Li-Ning Company, which manufactures sporting clothing and shoes. At the opening of the 2008 Games, he was given the honor of lighting the Olympic cauldron in a spectacular spin above the "Bird's Nest" stadium.

Bart Conner of the United States earned individual gold on the parallel bars, scoring a perfect 10—the first American individual gold on any gymnastic apparatus since 1932.

American Peter Vidmar won a gold medal in the individual pommel horse as well as the team gold medal. Moreover, he earned a silver medal in the closest men's all-around Olympic competition in 60 years. He thereby became the first American-born gymnast to medal in the individual all-around and the first to finish in the top eight since 1932.

Peter Vidmar remains the highest-scoring American gymnast in Olympic history.

Tracy Caulkins, captain of the United States women's swim team, won three gold medals. She set the Olympic record at 2:12.64 in the 200-meter individual medley. Her other golds were in the 400-meter individual medley and the 400-meter medley relay.

After setting the Olympic record in the 100-meter breaststroke at 1:09.88, Petra van Staveren of Holland (left) accepted congratulations from bronze medalist Catherine Poirot of France.

Mary Meagher of the United States won three gold medals at the Games swimming the butterfly: the individual 100-meter and 200-meter and the butterfly leg of the 4x100-meter medley relay. She won a bronze medal in the 200-meter butterfly at the Seoul 1988 Games.

Tiffany Cohen was a double gold medalist in the 400-meter and 800-meter freestyle races.

For many, the most memorable athlete of the Games was Mary Lou Retton of the United States. Her perfect 10s on the floor exercise and the vault in the final rotation, despite knee surgery five weeks earlier, confirmed her victory in the women's individual all-around competition. It was the first time a female gymnast outside of Eastern Europe won gold in that event. In all, Retton won five medals.

Mary Lou Retton was jubilantly greeted upon her all-around victory by her coach Bela Karolyi. Karolyi, who had coached 1976 and 1980 Olympic champion Nadia Comaneci, immigrated to the United States in 1981. In his illustrious career, he coached nine Olympic champions and 15 world champions.

Ecatarina Szabo of Romania exulted after winning her fifth medal in women's gymnastics. She took two gold medals and two silver medals for individual events plus Romania's gold medal for team competition.

Most equestrian events were held at Santa Anita Park in Arcadia. However, on August 1, the endurance test of the three-day event took place at Fairbanks Ranch in San Diego County, where 50,000 people attended. Part of the course passed through an "Old West Town."

The German road cycling team in the time trials had the rare treat of riding on a completely empty California freeway, the Artesia Freeway (I-91).

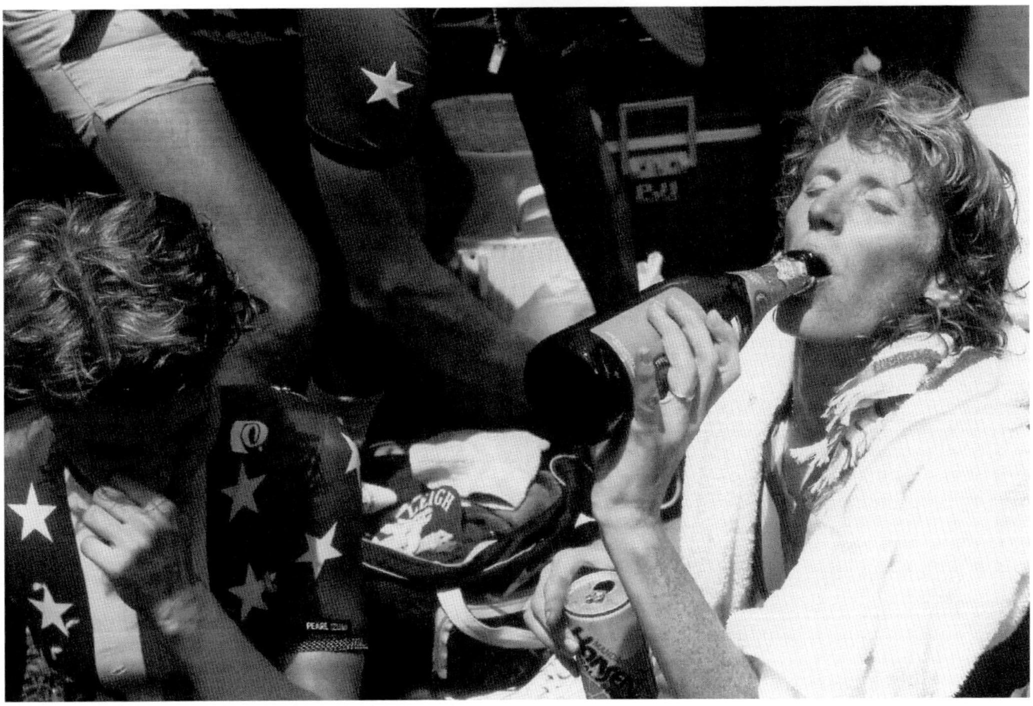

In Mission Viejo, the inaugural Olympic women's road race was won by Connie Carpenter-Phinney, who celebrated with champagne. American Carpenter-Phinney had been a speed skater on the 1972 Winter Olympic team in Sapporo at age 14. Carrying on a family tradition, her son Taylor Phinney competed on the United States cycling team at the Beijing 2008 Games and London 2012 Games.

Mark Gorski of the United States took the individual sprint gold medal at the Olympic velodrome.

The German team (left) won bronze in the 4,000-meter team pursuit. Australia and the United States came in first and second, respectively.

Rowing was held at Lake Casitas in Ventura County. Australia won gold in the eight oars with coxswain event.

Germany and the Netherlands competed in water polo at the Runnels Memorial Pool at Pepperdine University in Malibu (below). Yugoslavia, the United States, and Germany received the gold, silver, and bronze medals, respectively.

Rhythmic gymnastics made its Olympic debut at the Games at Pauley Pavilion at UCLA.

The men's kayak doubles (K-2) 1,000-meter competition was held at Lake Casitas in Ventura County. The winners were Canada, France, and Australia, in that order.

A total of 8,700 news media were accredited to the Games: 3,837 from the written and photographic press and 4,863 from electronic media. That compares to 7,078 athletes, or more than one journalist per athlete. The world's appetite for coverage of the Games was huge.

Over 5.7 million tickets were sold to the Games. The Coliseum filled daily for track-and-field events. The most surprising level of attendance was for the soccer competition at four venues around the country culminating in the Rose Bowl in Pasadena, which drew over 1.4 million attendees.

American sprinter and long jumper Carl Lewis was spectacular, matching Jesse Owens's 1936 record of four gold medals. He won gold in the 100-meter, 200-meter, and 4x100-meter races and in the long jump. These were his first Olympic medals on the way to a career total of nine gold medals.

Carl Lewis ran the 100-meter race in 9.99 seconds, one of 15 times in his career he covered that distance in less than 10 seconds.

Carl Lewis's long jump win was among his 65 consecutive victories in the event over a 10-year period—one of track and field's greatest records.

In 1999, two years after his retirement, the IOC named Carl Lewis "Sportsman of the Century."

Carl Lewis (right) won the 200-meter contest in an Olympic record time of 19.80 seconds. Kirk Baptiste (left) and Thomas Jefferson took silver and bronze for an American sweep.

Carl Lewis (left) anchored the world record setting 4x100-meter relay with Sam Graddy, Ron Brown, and Calvin Smith (right) in 37.83 seconds. After the Games, Graddy and Brown had careers in the National Football League. Smith continued to compete on the track. At the Seoul 1988 Games, he won a bronze medal in the controversial 100-meter race when Ben Johnson of Canada was disqualified for use of anabolic steroids.

Archery competition in El Dorado Park, Long Beach, featured Olympic history's first wheelchair-bound medal-event competitor, Neroli Fairhall of New Zealand. Darrell Pace of the United States and Hyang-Soon Seo of Korea won the men's and women's archery gold medals, respectively, setting Olympic records.

The United States women's basketball team, led by four-time college All-American Cheryl Miller, celebrated its gold medal win over Korea. The score of 85-55 was the closest game the undefeated American team had in the tournament. Beginning in 1984, the United States has won gold in women's basketball in every Olympic Games except the Barcelona 1992 Games, where it took bronze.

Gregory Louganis won both the springboard and platform diving golds in the Olympic pool at USC. When he repeated the feat in Seoul in 1988 he became the only male and the second diver in Olympic history to take both events in consecutive Olympic Games.

Gregory Louganis received the James E. Sullivan Award as the most outstanding amateur athlete in the United States in 1984.

The sailing competition was held off Long Beach harbor. Here, two sailors compete in the Flying Dutchman class, which was won by the United States.

Another landmark event at the 1984 Games was the first Olympic windgliding (windsurfing) competition. As part of the sailing program off Long Beach, 38 competitors from 38 nations took part. The reigning world champion, Stephan van den Berg of the Netherlands, took the gold.

The 1984 Games were the last for amateurs in Olympic basketball. Michael Jordan, 21 years old and not yet a professional, led a team that won all eight games by an average of 32 points. The team, coached by legendary Bobby Knight, also featured such great players as Patrick Ewing and Chris Mullin, who again appeared at the Olympic Games in 1992 with the first "Dream Team" of NBA players.

Synchronized swimming debuted at the Games. Below, Saeko Kimura and Miwako Motoyoshi of Japan swam to bronze medals in the duet event. The United States emerged victorious in the duet event, and Tracie Ruiz of the United States won the gold medal in the solo event.

Boxer Virgil Hill of the United States defeated Mohamed Zaoui of Algeria on his way to a silver medal in the middleweight division at the Los Angeles Memorial Sports Arena. Joon-Sup Shin of Korea won the gold. (Photograph by Robert Lachman, courtesy NOPP/ *LA Times*.)

Tyrell Biggs of the United States (right) defeated Francesco Damiani of Italy on points to take Olympics history's first super heavyweight crown. In the quarterfinals, Biggs had beaten Canadian Lennox Lewis, who later, as a professional, became the undisputed heavyweight world champion. Biggs also went on to a professional career from 1984 to 1998 in which he was a contender but never a champion.

American Willie Banks (left) competed in the triple jump, which was won by Al Joyner of the United States at 17.26 meters. Banks set the world record in 1985 with a jump of 17.97 meters and competed at the Olympics again at the Seoul 1988 Games. He served as president of U.S. Olympians from 2005 to 2008.

Daley Thompson of Great Britain took gold in the decathlon with an Olympic record 8,797 points. His victory was the crest of a continuing friendly rivalry with Juergen Hingsen of the Federal Republic of Germany, who came close with 8,673 points. Over the years, Thompson set the world record in the decathlon four times.

Ulrike Meyfarth of Germany leaped to a high jump Olympic record of 2.02 meters to take the gold with a Fosbury flop. In 1972 in Munich, at age 16, she had become the youngest woman to ever win Olympic gold in the high jump. In 1984, she became the oldest woman up to that date to garner the high jump championship.

An Olympic record of 69.56 meters was set by Tessa Sanderson of Great Britain in the javelin. She was the first woman from Britain to win this event at any Olympic Games. Sanderson competed in six Olympic Games from 1976 to 1996—one of only two track-and-field athletes ever to do so.

Brazilian Joaquim Cruz (left wearing No. 093) set an Olympic record of 1:43 in taking the 800-meter championship, beating Sebastian Coe of Great Britain and Earl Jones of the United States. He is still the only Brazilian to have won a gold medal on the running track.

American Edwin Moses gave a gold-medal performance in the 400-meter hurdles, beating German silver medalist Harald Schmid (right). Over 10 years, Moses won 107 consecutive finals (122 consecutive races) in the 400-meter hurdles and set the world record four times. As of 2013, he still holds 25 of the 100 fastest times in the event.

Britons Sebastian Coe (left) and Steve Cram finished first and second in the 1,500-meter race, with Coe's Olympic record time of 3:32.53. Coe, Cram, and their fellow Brit Steve Ovett dominated the middle distance throughout the 1980s. Coe went on to head the London bid for the 2012 Olympic Games and the London Organising Committee for the Olympic Games. He became chair of the British Olympic Association in 2012.

German equestrian athletes won gold medals in dressage in both the individual and team events at Santa Anita Park in Arcadia.

Joe Fargis of the United States on Touch of Class won gold in the individual jumping equestrian competition at Santa Anita Park in Arcadia.

Team handball was contested at the Titan Gymnasium at California State University Fullerton. Yugoslavia, Germany, and Romania won the gold, silver, and bronze medals, respectively, in the men's events.

Valerie Brisco-Hooks of the United States set Olympic records in both the 200-meter and 400-meter races and as a member of the 4x400-meter team and took three gold medals. She became the first to win gold medals in both the 200-meter and 400-meter races at a single Olympics—a record matched in subsequent Games by Michael Johnson of the United States and Marie-Jose Perec of France.

Evelyn Ashford of the United States sped to an Olympic record 10.97 seconds in the 100-meter. Ashford won another gold as a member of the 4x100-meter team, as she did in Seoul in 1988 and Barcelona in 1992. She is one of only four women in the history of track and field to win four gold medals. At the Seoul 1988 Games, she was honored by the USOC as the team's flag bearer in the Opening Ceremony.

The pre-race favorite, Mary Decker (center), was in the lead for the United States early in the 3,000-meter. Decker and her youthful challenger, the barefoot runner originally from banned apartheid South Africa (and running for Great Britain) Zola Budd (third from left), collided midway through the race. Decker did not finish. A bruised Budd came in seventh. Maricica Pulca of Romania won in Olympic record time of 8:35.96.

Mary Decker was carried off the track by her husband-to-be Richard Slaney.

Mexico exulted in the one-two finish of Ernesto Canto (right) and Raul Gonzalez in the 20-kilometer walk. The walking courses began and finished in the Coliseum, using a 2.5-kilometer loop course outside the Coliseum on Exposition Boulevard.

Raul Gonzalez donned a Mexican sombrero after setting an Olympic record, winning gold in the 50-kilometer walk event (31 miles) at 3:47:26.

Another innovation in Los Angeles was the women's 400-meter hurdles, won by Nawal El Moutawakel. She was the first Moroccan and the first woman from a Muslim-majority country to become an Olympic champion. She was also the first female Muslim born in Africa to win gold. She later became a vice president of the IOC as well as minister of sport of Morocco.

The American 4x400-meter team of, from left to right, Sherri Howard, Chandra Cheeseborough, Valerie Brisco-Hooks, and Lillie Leatherwood, set an Olympic record of 3:18.29. Cheeseborough became the first woman in Olympic history to win gold in both the 4x100-meter and 4x400-meter. No one matched this achievement until Allyson Felix of the United States at the London 2012 Games.

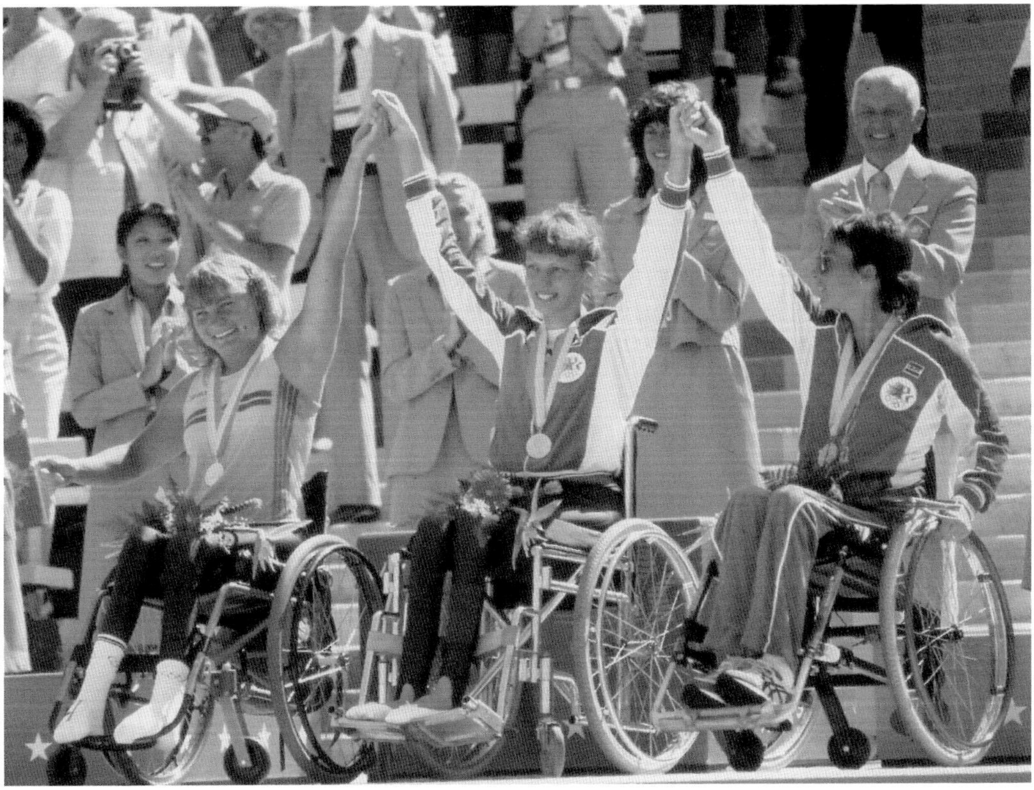

As an Olympic milestone, the 1984 Games added a women's and a men's wheelchair race as exhibitions. Being exhibition events, no official Olympic medals were awarded, but unofficial medals were given and the crowd rose to standing ovations in honor of the competitors. Sharon Hedrick (center) of the United States won the 800-meter women's event for a world record of 2:15.73. Monica Saker of Sweden (left) took silver, and Candace Cable of the United States earned bronze.

Paul van Winkel of Belgium won the inaugural 1,500-meter men's wheelchair race in the Coliseum. These exciting races were an important step toward the later embrace of the Paralympic Games by the IOC.

Left, Carsten Jensen of Denmark defeated Fabian Luis Lannutti of Argentina in a round of the half-heavyweight (95-kilogram) judo competition in the Eagle's Nest Arena at California State University Los Angeles. The event was won by Hyoung-Zoo Ha from Korea.

Steffi Graf of Germany beat Sabrina Goles of Yugoslavia to take the gold in the tennis exhibition matches at the Los Angeles Tennis Center at UCLA. In 1999, the IOC awarded Graf its highest honor, the Olympic Order. (Photograph by Tony Bernard, courtesy NOPP/*LA Times*.)

France beat Brazil to win the title in the soccer (football) tournament that finished at the Rose Bowl in Pasadena. The final game was attended by 101,799 people. Rolls of unprinted tickets had to be helicoptered into the Rose Bowl to sell to unanticipated walk-up buyers. The whole tournament, occurring across the nation, drew 1,422,605 people to the stadia. This was unexpected in a country thought to be indifferent to soccer.

This photograph was taken during France's (dark shirts) semifinal 4-2 victory over Yugoslavia in the Rose Bowl.

Gabi Andersen-Schiess, competing for Switzerland, gave one of the most dramatic and courageous performances of the Games as she entered the Coliseum for the last 400 meters of the marathon suffering from advanced heat exhaustion. She refused medical treatment to be able to complete the race in 37th place. Her lap around the Coliseum track took an excruciating five minutes and 44 seconds.

The winner of the first-ever Olympic women's marathon was Joan Benoit of the United States. She led through most of the race and finished in 2:24:52, almost a minute and a half and several hundred meters ahead of Grete Waitz of Norway (silver) and Rosa Mota of Portugal (bronze).

Ed Etzel of the United States won the gold medal in the small-bore rifle competition at the Prado Recreational Area in Chino. (Photograph by Larry Bessel, courtesy NOPP/*LA Times*.)

The precursor to the Closing Ceremony on the evening of August 12 was the men's marathon. Carlos Lopes entered the Coliseum to the roar of the crowd. He finished in Olympic record time of 2:09.21 with a 200-meter lead over the silver medalist, John Treacy of Ireland. Lopes became the first Portuguese athlete to win an Olympic gold medal.

At 8:00 p.m., the closing formalities began with presentation of the medals for the men's marathon and the equestrian individual jumping competition. The All-American Olympic Marching Band entered the stadium through the peristyle as the 140 flags of the teams were paraded into the stadium, followed by a half-hour entry of all the athletes as a single group (above). They took one last joyous victory lap. Then, in a ceremony, the Antwerp Olympic Flag was passed by IOC president Samaranch and Mayor Bradley to Seoul mayor Bo Hyun Yum. There were brief Korean and American dance presentations. LAOOC president Ueberroth and Samaranch spoke, declared the Games closed, and the Olympic flag was lowered and the flame extinguished. In the darkness, the audience was told to light the flashlights they had been given, whereupon a spaceship appeared to hover over the peristyle (below). The longest fireworks show in Olympic history to date, almost a half hour, ensued. (Photograph below by Jayne Kamin, courtesy NOPP/*LA Times*.)

Singer Lionel Richie appeared on the specially built stage and sang a newly arranged version of his hit song "All Night Long" for about 10 minutes along with break-dancers, water effects, and pyrotechnics.

The evening ended with a four-minute burst of grand finale fireworks. No one wanted to leave.

6

The Games Establish a Legacy

Neither the Olympic movement nor Los Angeles has been the same after the 1984 Games. By producing the Games in a manner that brought both glory and financial benefit to the host city and its national Olympic committee, Los Angeles reawakened interest among potential hosts worldwide. In 1986, six cities bid for the 1992 Olympic Games and seven cities bid for the 1992 Winter Games. Global interest in bidding for the Games and other major sporting events has not waned since. Los Angeles gave the movement blueprints it has consistently followed for professional management; television and exclusive sponsorship arrangements; torch relay revenue; armies of volunteers; and opening and closing ceremonies that are thrilling television extravaganzas. Other key elements of the Los Angeles Games, such as privately funded and managed Games and use of existing facilities (and Los Angeles's concomitant financial surplus) have yet to be reproduced.

The effect on Los Angeles was not physical; it was more important: it was a change in its perception by others and by itself. Many Angelenos who experienced those 16 days say they remember them as the most exciting days of their lives. The city gained a new confidence and a new reputation as a major world metropolis and cultural capital. The Olympic Arts Festival was followed by at least four other festivals patterned after its collaborative model.

Los Angeles became a frequent locale for world and national sports championships, including the 1994 FIFA World Cup Finals and the 1999 and 2003 FIFA Women's World Cup Finals, as well as the USOC's 1991 Olympic Festival and the IOC's 2012 Conference on Women in Sport. The city has continued to add new world-class sports venues through private initiatives. The financial surplus of 1984 still provides funds for the operations of the USOC and youth sports activities sponsored by the LA84 Foundation (formerly the Amateur Athletic Foundation). Los Angeles returned to bidding to be the USOC's candidate for the Games with its efforts for 2012, 2016, and 2024.

Moreover, the Olympic Games enhanced the sense of community for the residents of the astonishingly diverse 88 cities of Los Angeles County. The memory and accomplishments of the Olympic Games are the common inheritance of the people of Los Angeles.

A key legacy of the Games is the LA84 Foundation. Endowed with $100 million from the surplus of the Games, it supports youth sports and has one of the world's leading libraries and resource centers for sports. Its headquarters (left) is the historic Britt Mansion in the West Adams District, donated to the foundation by First Interstate Bank along with the sports memorabilia collection of Southern California Committee leader Paul Helms. (Photograph by author.)

Anita de Frantz, Olympic medalist in rowing, has led the LA84 Foundation as president since 1987. Previously, she was LAOOC vice president/athletes' villages. She was elected to the IOC in 1986 and has served as its first vice president. She was elected in 2013 to her second tenure on the IOC Executive Board. (Photograph by author.)

From its founding in 1985 through 2012, the LA84 Foundation committed more than $200 million to youth sports and sports research. To date, more than 3 million boys and girls and more than 1,100 youth sports organizations throughout Southern California have benefitted.

The foundation assists young people by grants to sports-related organizations and by its own programming, with a particular emphasis on underserved portions of the population. It supports varied activities from sports leagues to coaching clinics to swimming lessons.

An eternal Olympic flame burns at the headquarters of the LA84 Foundation in front of its Paul Ziffren Sports Resource Center. The center is one of the world's leading sports libraries, with an extensive print and digital collection of resources. It operates a Web site that offers vast digital information on sports and publishes papers and sponsors conferences on sports topics. It also maintains a major sports memorabilia collection. (Photograph by author.)

The LA84 Foundation has funded valuable capital projects related to sports in Southern California, such as the renovation of the Los Angeles Swimming Stadium (built for the 1932 Games) into a versatile recreation center called Expo Center and John C. Argue Swim Stadium, operated by the Los Angeles City Department of Recreation and Parks in Exposition Park (above), and the Rose Bowl Aquatics Center in Pasadena. (Photograph by author.)

Following the 1984 Games, the Los Angeles area continued to add new state-of-the-art sports venues. Staples Center in downtown (above), the StubHub Center in Carson (below), the Galen Center at USC, a rebuilt Pauley Pavilion at UCLA, and the Honda Center in Anaheim are homes to basketball, ice hockey and skating, volleyball, tennis, track and field, soccer, and cycling, among other disciplines. The nearby city of Lancaster added the National Soccer Center, the largest in the west, with 35 fields. The new American Sports Center in Anaheim, with 35 volleyball courts and 25 basketball courts, is the largest indoor court facility in the United States. It is home to the US national men's and women's volleyball teams. (Both, courtesy AEG.)

The ADT Event Center at StubHub Center (formerly Home Depot Center) in Carson opened in 2004. It replaced the outdoor velodrome used in the 1984 Games and is one of only two indoor velodromes in the United States. It hosted the 2005 UCI Track Cycling World Championships. (Courtesy AEG.)

The Olympic Arts Festival freeway mural project suffered the ravages of time. Beginning in 2011, the Mural Conservancy of Los Angeles has been restoring many of them. Here is the George Romero mural *Going to the Olympics* in restoration in 2013 on the 101 Freeway downtown. Kent Twitchell's mural *Seventh Street Altarpiece* has been resurrected under a bridge on the 101 Freeway near the Romero mural. (Photograph by author.)

The Olympics Arts Festival inspired a series of citywide festivals on the same collaborative model in which numerous Los Angeles arts organizations are tapped to work on a single theme. Right is a poster for the 1993 staging of the citywide Los Angeles Festival, which occurred in 1987, 1990, and 1993 as an outgrowth of the Olympic Games. (Courtesy Allison Sampson.)

Here is a scene from the opera *Gotterdammerung*, which completed the Los Angeles Opera's 2010 Ring Festival LA, in which 122 partner organizations joined with the opera company for 10 weeks of programming related to the work of Richard Wagner. The renowned Los Angeles Opera itself is a legacy of the Olympics Arts Festival in that it was founded in 1985, inspired by the 1984 visit of the Royal Opera of Covent Garden. (Photograph by Monika Rittershaus, courtesy Los Angeles Opera.)